Write
on
Track

Daily Language Workouts

FEATURING

Daily MUG Shot Sentences
Weekly MUG Shot Paragraphs
Writing Prompts
Writing Topics
Show-Me Sentences

Daily language and writing practice for
Grade 3

WRITE SOURCE®

GREAT SOURCE EDUCATION GROUP
a Houghton Mifflin Company
Wilmington, Massachusetts
www.greatsource.com

A Few Words About
Daily Language Workouts 3

Before you begin . . .

The activities in this book will help your students develop basic writing and language skills. You'll find three types of exercises on the following pages:

MUG Shot Sentences There are 175 sentences highlighting **m**echanics, **u**sage, and/or **g**rammar (MUG). There's one sentence for every day of the school year. For the first 15 weeks, focused sentences usually concentrate on one skill per week. Then the sentences for the final 20 weeks present a mixed review of errors, and students are asked to correct several types of errors in each sentence.

MUG Shot Paragraphs There are 35 weekly paragraphs. During the first 15 weeks, the paragraphs, like the sentences, usually focus on one type of mechanics, usage, or grammar error. The paragraphs for the final 20 weeks offer a mixed review of editing skills based on skills covered during each week of sentences.

Daily Writing Practice This section begins with **writing prompts** presented on pages that you can photocopy or place on an overhead projector. The prompts include thought-provoking topics and graphics designed to inspire expository, narrative, descriptive, persuasive, and creative writing. A discussion of daily journal writing introduces the lists of intriguing **writing topics.** Finally, the **Show-Me sentences** provide starting points for paragraphs, essays, and a wide variety of other writing forms.

Authors: Pat Sebranek and Dave Kemper

Printed in the United States of America

International Standard Book Number: 0-669-48233-1

1 2 3 4 5 6 7 8 9 10 -POO- 06 05 04 03 02 01

Table of Contents

Editing and Proofreading Marks

These symbols may be used to correct MUG Shot sentences and paragraphs.

Insert here.	$\wedge$	*them* take$_\wedge$home
Insert a comma or colon.	$\wedge\!\!,\;\;\wedge\!\!:$	Troy$_\wedge$Michigan
Insert a period.	⊙	Mrs⊙
Insert a question mark or an exclamation point.	$\overset{?}{\wedge}\;\;\overset{!}{\wedge}$	How about you$\overset{?}{\wedge}$
Capitalize a letter.	$/$ (or) ≡	T /toronto (or) toronto≡
Make a capital letter lowercase.	$/$	h /History
Replace or delete.	——	*cold* a ~~hot~~ day
Insert an apostrophe.	$\overset{9}{V}$	Bill$\overset{9}{V}$s
Insert quotation marks.	$\overset{66}{V}\;\;\overset{99}{V}$	$\overset{66}{V}$Wow!$\overset{99}{V}$
Use italics.	_____	Gowanus Dogs

MUG Shot Sentences

The MUG Shot sentences are designed to be used at the beginning of each class period as a quick and efficient way to review **m**echanics, **u**sage, and **g**rammar. Each sentence can be corrected and discussed in 3 to 5 minutes.

Mug Shot Sentence Organizer

Name _____ Date _____

Corrected Sentence:

_____

_____

_____

Corrected Sentence:

_____

_____

_____

Corrected Sentence:

_____

_____

_____

Corrected Sentence:

_____

_____

_____

Corrected Sentence:

_____

_____

_____

MUG Shot Sentences

Implementation and Evaluation

The first 15 weeks of MUG Shot sentences are focused sentences. The sentences for each week usually focus on one proofreading skill. The remaining 20 weeks of MUG Shot sentences provide mixed reviews of two or three different proofreading skills per sentence.

Implementation

On the days you use MUG Shot sentences, write the sentence on the board, and read it aloud to be sure students understand the sentence. Write the corrections on the board as volunteers provide them. (The students may use the proofreading marks on page iv.) Have each student explain his or her corrections and discuss the results. If you wish, then ask all students to write the corrected form in their notebooks.

Or you may write a sentence on the board at the beginning of the class period. Allow students time to read the sentence to themselves. (Make sure they understand the sentence.) Be sure to read each sentence aloud before students begin. Then have students correct each MUG Shot in a space reserved for them in their notebooks (or on a copy of the "MUG Shot Sentence Organizer" provided on page 2 of this book). Students may be supplied with a copy of the "Editing and Proofreading Marks" on page iv as a guide for marking changes to their MUG Shot sentences. Then have students in pairs or as a class discuss their corrections. Also make sure that each student understands why the corrections were made.

Each Friday, review the MUG Shots covered for the week. You might assign the MUG Shot paragraph that contains errors similar to the type students have worked on for the week. (See page 75.)

Evaluation

If you assign sentences daily, evaluate your students' work at the end of each week. We recommend that you give them a basic performance score for their work. This performance score might be based on having each sentence for that week written correctly in their language arts notebooks or on their MUG Shot organizers.

Note: In the MUG Shot sentences showing corrections for run-on sentences and sentence fragments, usually just one possible correction is shown. However, there are often a number of possible answers that would also be correct.

MUG Shot Sentences

4

Week 1: Focused Sentences

* **End Punctuation**

    Michael's family went out West last summer

* **End Punctuation**

    Did you hear about his adventure

* **End Punctuation**

    Michael and his sister Katie got lost in a canyon

* **End Punctuation**

    Katie stepped on a rattlesnake

* **End Punctuation**

    Their parents were so glad to find them before dark

Week 1: Corrected Sentences

* **End Punctuation**

    Michael's family went out West last summer⊙

* **End Punctuation**

    Did you hear about his adventure*?*∧

* **End Punctuation**

    Michael and his sister Katie got lost in a canyon⊙

* **End Punctuation**

    Katie stepped on a rattlesnake⊙ *(or) !*

* **End Punctuation**

    Their parents were so glad to find them before dark⊙

MUG Shot Sentences

Week 2: Focused Sentences

* **Period After an Initial and After an Abbreviation**

  Richard M Sherman and his brother Robert B Sherman wrote music for <u>The Tigger Movie</u>.

* **Period After an Initial and After an Abbreviation**

  Dr Yafait's office is on N Main St in Madison, Wisconsin.

* **Period After an Initial and After an Abbreviation**

  A A Milne is one of Ms Moy's favorite authors.

* **Period After an Initial and After an Abbreviation**

  Dan M Langford, Jr, is the son of Dan M Langford, Sr.

* **Period After an Initial and After an Abbreviation**

  Mrs Rose's bakery is on E Spice Ave.

Week 2: Corrected Sentences

* **Period After an Initial and After an Abbreviation**

  Richard M. Sherman and his brother Robert B. Sherman wrote music for <u>The Tigger Movie</u>.

* **Period After an Initial and After an Abbreviation**

  Dr. Yafait's office is on N. Main St. in Madison, Wisconsin.

* **Period After an Initial and After an Abbreviation**

  A. A. Milne is one of Ms. Moy's favorite authors.

* **Period After an Initial and After an Abbreviation**

  Dan M. Langford, Jr., is the son of Dan M. Langford, Sr.

* **Period After an Initial and After an Abbreviation**

  Mrs. Rose's bakery is on E. Spice Ave.

Week 3: Focused Sentences

* **Comma Between Items in a Series**

     Cheese yogurt and milk are all dairy products.

* **Comma Between Items in a Series**

     Elena likes to read books write letters and play the piano.

* **Comma Between Items in a Series**

     Jake has been to Michigan Indiana Ohio and Pennsylvania.

* **Comma Between Items in a Series**

     Mark will invite Rolando Joel Steve and Zach to his party.

* **Comma Between Items in a Series**

     Dad washes the car mows the lawn and plays with us.

MUG Shot Sentences

Week 3: Corrected Sentences

* **Comma Between Items in a Series**

Cheese, yogurt, and milk are all dairy products.

* **Comma Between Items in a Series**

Elena likes to read books, write letters, and play the piano.

* **Comma Between Items in a Series**

Jake has been to Michigan, Indiana, Ohio, and Pennsylvania.

* **Comma Between Items in a Series**

Mark will invite Rolando, Joel, Steve, and Zach to his party.

* **Comma Between Items in a Series**

Dad washes the car, mows the lawn, and plays with us.

MUG Shot Sentences

Week 4: Focused Sentences

* **Comma to Keep Numbers Clear**

   Troop 480 sold 1534 boxes of Girl Scout cookies this year.

* **Comma to Keep Numbers Clear**

   There are about 43000 people in our community.

* **Comma to Keep Numbers Clear**

   Mr. Hurst's antique car is worth between $30000 and $40000!

* **Comma to Keep Numbers Clear**

   We have more than 3500 books in our school library. The city library has more than 10000 books.

* **Comma to Keep Numbers Clear**

   Michigan Stadium can seat more than 106000 fans for a football game!

Week 4: Corrected Sentences

* Comma to Keep Numbers Clear

Troop 480 sold 1,534 boxes of Girl Scout cookies this year.

* Comma to Keep Numbers Clear

There are about 43,000 people in our community.

* Comma to Keep Numbers Clear

Mr. Hurst's antique car is worth between $30,000 and $40,000!

* Comma to Keep Numbers Clear

We have more than 3,500 books in our school library. The city library has more than 10,000 books.

* Comma to Keep Numbers Clear

Michigan Stadium can seat more than 106,000 fans for a football game!

MUG Shot Sentences

Week 5: Focused Sentences

* **Comma in Dates and Between a City and a State**

   Darrin wrote a letter to his Uncle Frank in Durham North Carolina.

* **Comma in Dates and Between a City and a State**

   He mailed the letter on June 14 2001.

* **Comma in Dates and Between a City and a State**

   Darrin now lives in Birmingham Michigan.

* **Comma in Dates and Between a City and a State**

   The letter was stamped at the post office in Royal Oak Michigan.

* **Comma in Dates and Between a City and a State**

   Uncle Frank received Darrin's letter on June 18 2001.

Week 5: Corrected Sentences

✸ **Comma in Dates and Between a City and a State**

Darrin wrote a letter to his Uncle Frank in Durham⌄North
Carolina.

✸ **Comma in Dates and Between a City and a State**

He mailed the letter on June 14⌄2001.

✸ **Comma in Dates and Between a City and a State**

Darrin now lives in Birmingham⌄Michigan.

✸ **Comma in Dates and Between a City and a State**

The letter was stamped at the post office in Royal Oak⌄Michigan.

✸ **Comma in Dates and Between a City and a State**

Uncle Frank received Darrin's letter on June 18⌄2001.

MUG Shot Sentences

Week 6: Focused Sentences

❋ Comma in Compound Sentences

I ate all my potatoes and I even tried some spinach.

❋ Comma in Compound Sentences

My sister hid her lima beans and our dog ate every one!

❋ Comma in Compound Sentences

My dad took us to see a movie but he didn't buy us any popcorn.

❋ Comma in Compound Sentences

Joey invited me to his house but I had too much homework to do.

❋ Comma in Compound Sentences

We could play basketball after school or we could go in-line skating.

Week 6: Corrected Sentences

✱ Comma in Compound Sentences

I ate all my potatoes‸and I even tried some spinach.

✱ Comma in Compound Sentences

My sister hid her lima beans‸and our dog ate every one!

✱ Comma in Compound Sentences

My dad took us to see a movie‸but he didn't buy us any popcorn.

✱ Comma in Compound Sentences

Joey invited me to his house‸but I had too much homework to do.

✱ Comma in Compound Sentences

We could play basketball after school‸or we could go in-line skating.

Week 7: Focused Sentences

✳ Comma to Set Off a Speaker's Words

Dad asked "Who wants to go for a bike ride?"

✳ Comma to Set Off a Speaker's Words

I yelled "I do, I do!"

✳ Comma to Set Off a Speaker's Words

"Don't forget to wear your helmet" Mom called.

✳ Comma to Set Off a Speaker's Words

I asked Dad "Can Victor come, too?"

✳ Comma to Set Off a Speaker's Words

"Yes" Dad answered. "Why don't you call him right now?"

Week 7: Corrected Sentences

✳ Comma to Set Off a Speaker's Words

Dad askedᴀ "Who wants to go for a bike ride?"

✳ Comma to Set Off a Speaker's Words

I yelledᴀ "I do, I do!"

✳ Comma to Set Off a Speaker's Words

"Don't forget to wear your helmetᴀ" Mom called.

✳ Comma to Set Off a Speaker's Words

I asked Dadᴀ "Can Victor come, too?"

✳ Comma to Set Off a Speaker's Words

"Yesᴀ" Dad answered. "Why don't you call him right now?"

MUG Shot Sentences

Week 8: Focused Sentences

* **Comma After an Introductory Word**

   "Denise can you help me untie this knot?"

* **Comma After an Introductory Word**

   "Goodness that was a loud bang!"

* **Comma After an Introductory Group of Words**

   "When you're done reading that book may I read it?"

* **Comma After an Introductory Group of Words**

   While we were sleeping a raccoon got into the garbage.

* **Comma After an Introductory Word**

   "Hey I can do that trick, too!"

Week 8: Corrected Sentences

✱ **Comma After an Introductory Word**

"Denise₍,₎ can you help me untie this knot?"

✱ **Comma After an Introductory Word**

"Goodness₍,₎ that was a loud bang!"

✱ **Comma After an Introductory Group of Words**

"When you're done reading that book₍,₎ may I read it?"

✱ **Comma After an Introductory Group of Words**

While we were sleeping₍,₎ a raccoon got into the garbage.

✱ **Comma After an Introductory Word**

"Hey₍,₎ I can do that trick, too!"

Week 9: Focused Sentences

* **Comma Between Describing Words**

   Nadia's poodle has short curly hair.

* **Comma Between Describing Words**

   Peter's cat has long silky fur.

* **Comma Between Describing Words**

   I love the sweet tart taste of caramel apples.

* **Comma Between Describing Words**

   Raul and Bryce gobbled up the hot spicy pizza.

* **Comma Between Describing Words**

   We live on a wide shady street.

Week 9: Corrected Sentences

✱ Comma Between Describing Words

Nadia's poodle has short, curly hair.

✱ Comma Between Describing Words

Peter's cat has long, silky fur.

✱ Comma Between Describing Words

I love the sweet, tart taste of caramel apples.

✱ Comma Between Describing Words

Raul and Bryce gobbled up the hot, spicy pizza.

✱ Comma Between Describing Words

We live on a wide, shady street.

Week 10: Focused Sentences

* **Colon**

  We eat lunch at 1130 a.m.

* **Colon**

  Dear Mr. Mayer

  Thank you for visiting our classroom.

* **Colon**

  I had to do three chores on Saturday walk the dog, unload the dishwasher, and help with the laundry.

* **Colon**

  Our baseball games always start at 730.

* **Colon**

  My brother has three friends Benjamin, David, and Logan.

Week 10: Corrected Sentences

* **Colon**

  We eat lunch at 11:30 a.m.

* **Colon**

  Dear Mr. Mayer:

  Thank you for visiting our classroom.

* **Colon**

  I had to do three chores on Saturday: walk the dog, unload the

  dishwasher, and help with the laundry.

* **Colon**

  Our baseball games always start at 7:30.

* **Colon**

  My brother has three friends: Benjamin, David, and Logan.

MUG Shot Sentences

Week 11: Focused Sentences

✳ **Apostrophe in Contractions**

Its time for recess.

✳ **Apostrophe in Contractions**

I think youre a great friend!

✳ **Apostrophe in Contractions**

Alaska wasnt the fiftieth state to join the union.

✳ **Apostrophe in Contractions**

I dont like doing chores, but I always get them done.

✳ **Apostrophe in Contractions**

The boys think theyre going to win the race.

Week 11: Corrected Sentences

* **Apostrophe in Contractions**

 It's time for recess.

* **Apostrophe In Contractions**

 I think you're a great friend!

* **Apostrophe in Contractions**

 Alaska wasn't the fiftieth state to join the union.

* **Apostrophe in Contractions**

 I don't like doing chores, but I always get them done.

* **Apostrophe in Contractions**

 The boys think they're going to win the race.

Week 12: Focused Sentences

---

* **Apostrophe to Form Possessives (Ownership)**

  Kyles bicycle is blue and red.

* **Apostrophe to Form Possessives (Ownership)**

  Yesterday I rode in Seans go-cart.

* **Apostrophe to Form Possessives (Ownership)**

  Nicole had to use Ramas spelling book to study her words.

* **Apostrophe to Form Possessives (Ownership)**

  Our neighbors garden is full of tomatoes!

* **Apostrophe to Form Possessives (Ownership)**

  My teachers first name is a secret.

Week 12: Corrected Sentences

✱ **Apostrophe to Form Possessives (Ownership)**

Kyle's bicycle is blue and red.

✱ **Apostrophe to Form Possessives (Ownership)**

Yesterday I rode in Sean's go-cart.

✱ **Apostrophe to Form Possessives (Ownership)**

Nicole had to use Rama's spelling book to study her words.

✱ **Apostrophe to Form Possessives (Ownership)**

Our neighbor's garden is full of tomatoes!

✱ **Apostrophe to Form Possessives (Ownership)**

My teacher's first name is a secret.

Week 13: Focused Sentences

＊ Apostrophe to Form Possessives (Ownership)

The boys team finished second in the three-legged race.

＊ Apostrophe to Form Possessives (Ownership)

The childrens choir sang in the concert.

＊ Apostrophe to Form Possessives (Ownership)

My friends names are Lakeshia and Nadine.

＊ Apostrophe to Form Possessives (Ownership)

The womens locker room is down the hall.

＊ Apostrophe to Form Possessives (Ownership)

I saw two swans nests near the lake.

MUG Shot Sentences

Week 13: Corrected Sentences

* **Apostrophe to Form Possessives (Ownership)**

   The boys᾽ team finished second in the three-legged race.

* **Apostrophe to Form Possessives (Ownership)**

   The children᾽s choir sang in the concert.

* **Apostrophe to Form Possessives (Ownership)**

   My friends᾽ names are Lakeshia and Nadine.

* **Apostrophe to Form Possessives (Ownership)**

   The women᾽s locker room is down the hall.

* **Apostrophe to Form Possessives (Ownership)**

   I saw two swans᾽ nests near the lake.

Week 14: Focused Sentences

---

* **Quotation Marks to Set Off Spoken Words**

   Let's go to the beach today, Mom said.

* **Quotation Marks to Set Off Spoken Words**

   Hooray, my sister and brother yelled.

* **Quotation Marks to Set Off Spoken Words**

   Mom said, We need to clear away the breakfast dishes.

* **Quotation Marks to Set Off Spoken Words**

   I'll get the dishcloth to wipe the table, I called.

* **Quotation Marks to Set Off Spoken Words**

   Great, Mom said. I'll pack our beach bag, and then we can go!

Week 14: Corrected Sentences

* **Quotation Marks to Set Off Spoken Words**

   "Let's go to the beach today," Mom said.

* **Quotation Marks to Set Off Spoken Words**

   "Hooray," my sister and brother yelled.

* **Quotation Marks to Set Off Spoken Words**

   Mom said, "We need to clear away the breakfast dishes."

* **Quotation Marks to Set Off Spoken Words**

   "I'll get the dishcloth to wipe the table," I called.

* **Quotation Marks to Set Off Spoken Words**

   "Great," Mom said. "I'll pack our beach bag, and then we can go!"

MUG Shot Sentences

Week 15: Focused Sentences

* **Quotation Marks to Punctuate Titles**

  The Homework Machine is one of my favorite poems.

* **Italics and Underlining**

  Tarzan and 102 Dalmatians are my favorite movies.

* **Quotation Marks to Punctuate Titles**

  We all sang The Star-Spangled Banner before the game began.

* **Italics and Underlining**

  National Geographic World is an awesome magazine for kids.

* **Italics and Underlining**

  Beverly Cleary wrote Ramona the Pest and many other children's

  books.

MUG Shot Sentences

Week 15: Corrected Sentences

* **Quotation Marks to Punctuate Titles**

"The Homework Machine" is one of my favorite poems.

* **Italics and Underlining**

<u>Tarzan</u> and <u>102 Dalmatians</u> are my favorite movies.

* **Quotation Marks to Punctuate Titles**

We all sang "The Star-Spangled Banner" before the game began.

* **Italics and Underlining**

<u>National Geographic World</u> is an awesome magazine for kids.

* **Italics and Underlining**

Beverly Cleary wrote <u>Ramona the Pest</u> and many other children's books.

MUG Shot Sentences

Week 16: Mixed-Review Sentences

Planets

* **Comma Between Items in a Series, Capitalization**

    Mercury venus earth and mars are all planets.

* **Comma in Compound Sentences, Capitalization**

    A year on Earth is 365 days long but a year on mercury is only 88 days long.

* **Apostrophe in Contractions, Using the Right Word**

    I wouldnt go to Pluto because its two cold and too far away.

* **Capitalization, Subject-Verb Agreement, End Punctuation**

    Did you know that both saturn and uranus has rings

* **Adjective (Form), Apostrophe to Form Possessives (Ownership)**

    Our atmosphere is more better than Jupiters atmosphere.

Week 16: Corrected Sentences

* **Comma Between Items in a Series, Capitalization**

   Mercury, Venus, Earth, and Mars are all planets.

* **Comma in Compound Sentences, Capitalization**

   A year on Earth is 365 days long, but a year on Mercury is only

   88 days long.

* **Apostrophe in Contractions, Using the Right Word**

   I wouldn't go to Pluto because it's two too cold and too far away.

* **Capitalization, Subject-Verb Agreement, End Punctuation**

   Did you know that both Saturn and Uranus has have rings?

* **Adjective (Form), Apostrophe to Form Possessives (Ownership)**

   Our atmosphere is more better than Jupiter's atmosphere.

MUG Shot Sentences

Week 17: Mixed-Review Sentences

Using Maps 1

* **Apostrophe in Contractions, Using the Right Word, Capitalization**

   Youll want to pack warm close if you go to alaska in the winter.

* **Capitalization, Colon, Comma Between Items in a Series**

   Three oceans surround north america the arctic the pacific and the atlantic.

* **Using the Right Word, Capitalization, Run-On Sentence**

   My family drove threw six states to get to florida that was the greatest vacation I ever had.

* **Capitalization, Run-On Sentence, Apostrophe in Contractions**

   The largest American desert is the mojave its in the state of california.

* **Comma Between Describing Words and to Set Off a Speaker's Words, Quotation Marks to Set Off Spoken Words**

   Lake Superior is a cold beautiful lake said the park ranger.

Week 17: Corrected Sentences

✳ **Apostrophe in Contractions, Using the Right Word, Capitalization**

You'll want to pack warm ~~close~~ *clothes* if you go to *A*laska in the winter.

✳ **Capitalization, Colon, Comma Between Items in a Series**

Three oceans surround *N*orth *A*merica: the *A*rctic, the *P*acific, and the *A*tlantic.

✳ **Using the Right Word, Capitalization, Run-On Sentence**

My family drove ~~threw~~ *through* six states to get to *F*lorida. *T*hat was the greatest vacation I ever had.

✳ **Capitalization, Run-On Sentence, Apostrophe in Contractions**

The largest American desert is the *M*ojave. *I*t's in the state of *C*alifornia.

✳ **Comma Between Describing Words and to Set Off a Speaker's Words, Quotation Marks to Set Off Spoken Words**

"Lake Superior is a cold, beautiful lake," said the park ranger.

MUG Shot Sentences

Week 18: Mixed-Review Sentences

Using Maps 2

✱ **Comma Between a City and a State and in Compound Sentences**

Miguel received a postcard from Key West Florida and it had a picture of palm trees on the front.

✱ **Subject-Verb Agreement, Comma in Compound Sentences, Capitalization**

We was in Utah on our vacation and we floated in the great salt lake.

✱ **Capitalization, Run-On Sentence, Comma to Keep Numbers Clear**

Rhode island is the smallest state it has only 1214 square miles.

✱ **Comma After an Introductory Word and to Keep Numbers Clear**

Wow Alaska has a mountain that is 20320 feet high.

✱ **Subject-Verb Agreement, Capitalization, End Punctuation**

Do you knows that the mississippi river is 2,340 miles long

MUG Shot Sentences

Week 18: Corrected Sentences

✱ **Comma Between a City and a State and in Compound Sentences**

Miguel received a postcard from Key West, Florida, and it had a picture of palm trees on the front.

✱ **Subject-Verb Agreement, Comma in Compound Sentences, Capitalization**

We ~~was~~ *were* in Utah on our vacation, and we floated in the ~~g~~*G*reat ~~s~~*S*alt ~~l~~*L*ake.

✱ **Capitalization, Run-On Sentence, Comma to Keep Numbers Clear**

Rhode ~~i~~*I*sland is the smallest state. ~~i~~*I*t has only 1,214 square miles.

✱ **Comma After an Introductory Word and to Keep Numbers Clear**

Wow, Alaska has a mountain that is 20,320 feet high.

✱ **Subject-Verb Agreement, Capitalization, End Punctuation**

Do you ~~knows~~ *know* that the ~~m~~*M*ississippi ~~r~~*R*iver is 2,340 miles long?

MUG Shot Sentences

Week 19: Mixed-Review Sentences

U.S. History 1

* **Capitalization, Comma in Dates**

  The Declaration of independence was signed on July 4 1776.

* **Capitalization, Comma in Compound Sentences, Numbers**

  The civil war started in 1861 and it ended 5 years later in 1865.

* **Using the Right Word, Capitalization**

  Pioneers crossed many rivers and creaks as they traveled to oregon and california.

* **Subject-Verb Agreement, Capitalization**

  Children does not go to school on saturdays.

* **Using the Right Word, Comma in Compound Sentences**

  It is now common to sea airplanes in the sky but in 1903 airplanes were brand-new.

Week 19: Corrected Sentences

* **Capitalization, Comma in Dates**

  The Declaration of *I*/independence was signed on July 4ˏ1776.

* **Capitalization, Comma in Compound Sentences, Numbers**

  The *C*/civil *W*/war started in 1861ˏand it ended *five*/5̶ years later in 1865.

* **Using the Right Word, Capitalization**

  Pioneers crossed many rivers and *creeks*/c̶r̶e̶a̶k̶s̶ as they traveled to *O*/oregon and *C*/california.

* **Subject-Verb Agreement, Capitalization**

  Children *do*/d̶o̶e̶s̶ not go to school on *S*/saturdays.

* **Using the Right Word, Comma in Compound Sentences**

  It is now common to *see*/s̶e̶a̶ airplanes in the skyˏbut in 1903 airplanes were brand-new.

Week 20: Mixed-Review Sentences

U.S. History 2

* **Colon, Comma Between Items in a Series**

   Here are some inventions that changed our world telephones airplanes and rockets.

* **Period After an Abbreviation, Capitalization, Run-On Sentence**

   Martin Luther King, jr, fought for civil rights he believed everyone should be treated fairly.

* **Comma After an Introductory Group of Words, Verb (Irregular), Capitalization**

   When he flown across the atlantic ocean in 1927 Charles Lindbergh became a hero.

* **Using the Right Word, Period After an Abbreviation, End Punctuation**

   Did you no there is a US flag on the moon

* **Capitalization, Numbers, End Punctuation**

   Are Alaska and hawaii our 2 newest states

Week 20: Corrected Sentences

✻ Colon, Comma Between Items in a Series

Here are some inventions that changed our world : telephones , airplanes , and rockets.

✻ Period After an Abbreviation, Capitalization, Run-On Sentence

Martin Luther King, *Jr.,* fought for civil rights. *H*e believed everyone should be treated fairly.

✻ Comma After an Introductory Group of Words, Verb (Irregular), Capitalization

When he *flew* ~~flown~~ across the *A*tlantic *O*cean in 1927 , Charles Lindbergh became a hero.

✻ Using the Right Word, Period After an Abbreviation, End Punctuation

Did you *know* ~~no~~ there is a U.S. flag on the moon ?

✻ Capitalization, Numbers, End Punctuation

Are Alaska and *H*awaii our *two* ~~2~~ newest states ?

MUG Shot Sentences

Week 21: Mixed-Review Sentences

Using Reference Materials 1

* **Quotation Marks to Set Off Spoken Words, Period After an Abbreviation, Comma Between Items in a Series**

  Encyclopedias dictionaries and atlases are all reference books, said Ms Waters.

* **Plurals, Capitalization, Comma in Compound Sentences**

  Leroy looked for two biographys of thomas edison but he found only one.

* **Comma to Set Off a Speaker's Words, Italics and Underlining, Quotation Marks to Set Off Spoken Words**

  Mrs. Santos said Look in a book called From Sea to Shining Sea for facts about the states.

* **Capitalization, Italics and Underlining**

  If you have to do a report on france or spain, look for information in the World Almanac or in an encyclopedia.

* **Apostrophe to Form Possessives (Ownership), Subject-Verb Agreement**

  Hillarys favorite part of the library are the nonfiction section.

Week 21: Corrected Sentences

* **Quotation Marks to Set Off Spoken Words, Period After an Abbreviation, Comma Between Items in a Series**

    "Encyclopedias, dictionaries, and atlases are all reference books," said Ms. Waters.

* **Plurals, Capitalization, Comma in Compound Sentences**

    Leroy looked for two ~~biographys~~ *biographies* of thomas edison, but he found only one.

* **Comma to Set Off a Speaker's Words, Italics and Underlining, Quotation Marks to Set Off Spoken Words**

    Mrs. Santos said, "Look in a book called From Sea to Shining Sea for facts about the states."

* **Capitalization, Italics and Underlining**

    If you have to do a report on france or spain, look for information in the World Almanac or in an encyclopedia.

* **Apostrophe to Form Possessives (Ownership), Subject-Verb Agreement**

    Hillarys favorite part of the library ~~are~~ *is* the nonfiction section.

MUG Shot Sentences

Week 22: Mixed-Review Sentences

Using Reference Materials 2

✱ Capitalization, Comma Between Items in a Series, End Punctuation

the table of contents the glossary and the index help you find information in books

✱ Period After an Abbreviation, Italics and Underlining, Capitalization

Dr Seuss is the author of Green eggs and Ham.

✱ Using the Right Word, Comma in Compound Sentences

I waited four my turn on the computer but the bell rang before I could use it.

✱ Subject-Verb Agreement, Run-On Sentence, Comma in Dates

Benji were born on December 25 1992 he has a birthday party in the summer.

✱ Comma After an Introductory Word and in Dates, Quotation Marks to Set Off Spoken Words

Bruce shouted, Wow I found a book that was first checked out on March 15 1947!

MUG Shot Sentences

Week 22: Corrected Sentences

✳ Capitalization, Comma Between Items in a Series, End Punctuation

T
The table of contents, the glossary, and the index help you find information in books.

✳ Period After an Abbreviation, Italics and Underlining, Capitalization

E
Dr. Seuss is the author of Green eggs and Ham.

✳ Using the Right Word, Comma in Compound Sentences

for
I waited four my turn on the computer, but the bell rang before I could use it.

✳ Subject-Verb Agreement, Run-On Sentence, Comma in Dates

was *H*
Benji were born on December 25, 1992. he has a birthday party in the summer.

✳ Comma After an Introductory Word and in Dates, Quotation Marks to Set Off Spoken Words

Bruce shouted, "Wow, I found a book that was first checked out on March 15, 1947!"

MUG Shot Sentences

Week 23: Mixed-Review Sentences

A History of the Language 1

✳ **Using the Right Word, Capitalization, End Punctuation**

Do you know wear the english language came from

✳ **Capitalization, Comma Between Items in a Series and After an Introductory Group of Words**

Since english developed in Europe there are french german and spanish words in our language.

✳ **Capitalization, Run-On Sentence**

Some english words become part of other languages the word "weekend" means the same in french and english.

✳ **Comma Between Items in a Series, Capitalization, End Punctuation**

We learned animal names such as moose opossum and chipmunk from native Americans

✳ **Using the Right Word, Comma in Compound Sentences, Capitalization**

I never new that "alphabet" was a greek word but I do know that "pizza" is italian!

Week 23: Corrected Sentences

* **Using the Right Word, Capitalization, End Punctuation**

  Do you know ~~wear~~ *where* the ~~e~~*E*nglish language came from~~.~~?

* **Capitalization, Comma Between Items in a Series and After an Introductory Group of Words**

  Since ~~e~~*E*nglish developed in Europe, there are ~~f~~*F*rench, ~~g~~*G*erman, and ~~s~~*S*panish words in our language.

* **Capitalization, Run-On Sentence**

  Some ~~e~~*E*nglish words become part of other languages. ~~t~~*T*he word "weekend" means the same in ~~f~~*F*rench and ~~e~~*E*nglish.

* **Comma Between Items in a Series, Capitalization, End Punctuation**

  We learned animal names such as moose, opossum, and chipmunk from ~~n~~*N*ative Americans.

* **Using the Right Word, Comma in Compound Sentences, Capitalization**

  I never ~~new~~ *knew* that "alphabet" was a ~~g~~*G*reek word, but I do know that "pizza" is ~~i~~*I*talian!

MUG Shot Sentences

Week 24: Mixed-Review Sentences

A History of the Language 2

✳ **Capitalization, Using the Right Word**

the first printed books were maid in london in the 1400s.

✳ **Capitalization, Using the Right Word, Sentence Fragment**

The spanish added some of there words to the english language Cigar, canyon, and rodeo.

✳ **Quotation Marks to Punctuate Titles, Subject-Verb Agreement, Capitalization**

We sings the french song Frère Jacques in music class.

✳ **Apostrophe in Contractions, Run-On Sentence**

Its interesting to watch deaf people use sign language their hands move so quickly!

✳ **Capitalization, Comma in Compound Sentences**

Louis braille became blind as a child and he later invented the Braille alphabet.

Week 24: Corrected Sentences

✴ **Capitalization, Using the Right Word**

The first printed books were ~~maid~~ *made* in /London in the 1400s. *(T capitalized, made, L capitalized)*

✴ **Capitalization, Using the Right Word, Sentence Fragment**

The /Spanish added some of ~~there~~ *their* words to the /English language. *(or)* language. They are cigar, . . . /Cigar, canyon, and rodeo.

✴ **Quotation Marks to Punctuate Titles, Subject-Verb Agreement, Capitalization**

We ~~sings~~ *sing* the /French song "Frère Jacques" in music class.

✴ **Apostrophe in Contractions, Run-On Sentence**

It's interesting to watch deaf people use sign language. Their hands move so quickly!

✴ **Capitalization, Comma in Compound Sentences**

Louis /Braille became blind as a child, and he later invented the Braille alphabet.

MUG Shot Sentences

Week 25: Mixed-Review Sentences

A History of the Language 3

✱ **Using the Right Word, Comma to Keep Numbers Clear, Capitalization**

Their are more than 500000 words in the english language.

✱ **Capitalization, Italics and Underlining**

The little Prince is a famous french book.

✱ **Apostrophe in Contractions, Capitalization, Plurals**

Its hard for students from other countrys to learn english as a second language.

✱ **Comma Between Items in a Series, Run-On Sentence**

Words such as *through though* and *tough* are hard to learn they look like they should rhyme.

✱ **Capitalization, Sentence Fragment**

You feel the braille alphabet with your fingers. Need special tools to write in braille.

Week 25: Corrected Sentences

---

* **Using the Right Word, Comma to Keep Numbers Clear, Capitalization**

  There
  ~~Their~~ are more than 500,000 words in the ~~e~~nglish language.

  (E)

* **Capitalization, Italics and Underlining**

  (L)   (F)
  The little Prince is a famous french book.

* **Apostrophe in Contractions, Capitalization, Plurals**

  (')   *countries*   (E)
  Its hard for students from other ~~countrys~~ to learn english as a

  second language.

* **Comma Between Items in a Series, Run-On Sentence**

                                                              (T)
  Words such as *through*, *though*, and *tough* are hard to learn. they

  look like they should rhyme.

* **Capitalization, Sentence Fragment**

              (B)   *You n*
  You feel the braille alphabet with your fingers. Need special tools

         (B)
  to write in braille.

MUG Shot Sentences

Week 26: Mixed-Review Sentences

Greetings

* **Quotation Marks to Set Off Spoken Words,
  Comma to Set Off a Speaker's Words**

  Bonjour said the French visitor.

* **Quotation Marks to Set Off Spoken Words,
  Comma to Set Off a Speaker's Words**

  Adios called Juan as he walked away.

* **Using the Right Word, Capitalization**

  I think ant carla speaks italian very well.

* **Capitalization, Italics and Underlining**

  Children can learn spanish and english words while watching
  sesame street.

* **Using the Right Word, Capitalization**

  Joe knows how to right sentences in english and italian.

Week 26: Corrected Sentences

**✱ Quotation Marks to Set Off Spoken Words,
Comma to Set Off a Speaker's Words**

"Bonjour," said the French visitor.

**✱ Quotation Marks to Set Off Spoken Words,
Comma to Set Off a Speaker's Words**

"Adios," called Juan as he walked away.

✱ Using the Right Word, Capitalization

I think ~~ant~~ *Aunt* ~~c~~ *C*arla speaks ~~i~~ *I*talian very well.

✱ Capitalization, Italics and Underlining

Children can learn ~~s~~ *S*panish and ~~e~~ *E*nglish words while watching
~~s~~ *S*esame ~~s~~ *S*treet.

✱ Using the Right Word, Capitalization

Joe knows how to ~~right~~ *write* sentences in ~~e~~ *E*nglish and ~~i~~ *I*talian.

55

Week 27: Mixed-Review Sentences

Measurement

✳ **Using the Right Word, Capitalization**

Sixteen ounces equal won pound in the united states system of measurement.

✳ **Comma Between Items in a Series, End Punctuation**

The metric system is used in medicine science and some other areas

✳ **Using the Right Word, Numbers**

A paper clip ways about 1 gram.

✳ **Quotation Marks to Set Off Spoken Words, Hyphen**

There are about two and one half centimeters in one inch, said Mr. Anderson.

✳ **Comma After an Introductory Group of Words, Sentence Fragment, Apostrophe in Contractions**

If you dont have a ruler use a quarter to measure something small. Close to one inch wide.

MUG Shot Sentences

Week 27: Corrected Sentences

* **Using the Right Word, Capitalization**

  Sixteen ounces equal ~~won~~ *one* pound in the ~~u~~*U*nited ~~s~~*S*tates system of measurement.

* **Comma Between Items in a Series, End Punctuation**

  The metric system is used in medicine, science, and some other areas.

* **Using the Right Word, Numbers**

  A paper clip ~~ways~~ *weighs* about ~~1~~ *one* gram.

* **Quotation Marks to Set Off Spoken Words, Hyphen**

  "There are about two and one-half centimeters in one inch," said Mr. Anderson.

* **Comma After an Introductory Group of Words, Sentence Fragment, Apostrophe in Contractions**

  If you don't have a ruler, use a quarter to measure something small. *A quarter is c*~~C~~lose to one inch wide.

MUG Shot Sentences

Week 28: Mixed-Review Sentences

Graphics 1

* **Comma Between Items in a Series and in Compound Sentences**

    Tables symbols and diagrams are kinds of graphics and they can help you learn.

* **Using the Right Word, Sentence Fragment**

    The heart symbol stands four a feeling. Means love.

* **Using the Right Word, Comma Between Items in a Series**

    Blue rode signs usually mean that food gas or medical care is near.

* **Subject-Verb Agreement, Plurals**

    We draws diagrams of butterflys and frogs in science class.

* **Using the Right Word, Comma in Compound Sentences**

    Jim and Eric labeled there diagram and they colored it with bright colors.

Week 28: Corrected Sentences

* **Comma Between Items in a Series and in Compound Sentences**

    Tables$_{,}$ symbols$_{,}$ and diagrams are kinds of graphics$_{,}$ and they can help you learn.

* **Using the Right Word, Sentence Fragment**

    The heart symbol stands ~~four~~ *for* a feeling.$_\wedge$ ~~M~~eans love.
    It m

* **Using the Right Word, Comma Between Items in a Series**

    Blue ~~rode~~ *road* signs usually mean that food$_{,}$ gas$_{,}$ or medical care is near.

* **Subject-Verb Agreement, Plurals**

    We ~~draws~~ *draw* diagrams of ~~butterflys~~ *butterflies* and frogs in science class.

* **Using the Right Word, Comma in Compound Sentences**

    Jim and Eric labeled ~~there~~ *their* diagram$_{,}$ and they colored it with bright colors.

MUG Shot Sentences

Week 29: Mixed-Review Sentences

Graphics 2

* **Numbers, Run-On Sentence**

   Alyssa took a survey of thirty-five students then she made a table to organize the information.

* **Rambling Sentence, Apostrophe in Contractions**

   Five kids have fish and four kids have hamsters and eight kids have dogs and three kids dont have any pets.

* **Subject-Verb Agreement, Sentence Fragment**

   A table are an easy way to find facts. Has rows and columns.

* **Quotation Marks to Set Off Spoken Words, Comma After an Introductory Word**

   Mark please tell us what's for lunch today, said Ms. Romano.

* **Capitalization, Comma Between Items in a Series, End Punctuation**

   tables can use words numbers and symbols to tell information

Week 29: Corrected Sentences

* **Numbers, Run-On Sentence**

Alyssa took a survey of ~~thirty-five~~ *35* students. *T*then she made a table to organize the information.

* **Rambling Sentence, Apostrophe in Contractions**

Five kids have fish, ~~and~~ four kids have hamsters, and eight kids have dogs. ~~and~~ *T*three kids don't have any pets.

* **Subject-Verb Agreement, Sentence Fragment**

A table ~~are~~ *is* an easy way to find facts. *It h*Has rows and columns.

* **Quotation Marks to Set Off Spoken Words, Comma After an Introductory Word**

"Mark, please tell us what's for lunch today," said Ms. Romano.

* **Capitalization, Comma Between Items in a Series, End Punctuation**

*T*tables can use words, numbers, and symbols to tell information.

MUG Shot Sentences

Week 30: Mixed-Review Sentences

Graphics 3

✱ **Italics and Underlining, Comma Between Items in a Series**

TV Guide gives a table of times channels and programs for each night.

✱ **Italics and Underlining, Capitalization, Colon**

We looked in the paper to see if good morning america was on at 700 or 800.

✱ **Quotation Marks to Set Off Spoken Words, Comma to Set Off a Speaker's Words**

My little sister can read a stop sign bragged Matthew.

✱ **Subject-Verb Agreement, Apostrophe in Contractions**

Sue and Beth is going to the movies, and theyll come right home afterward.

✱ **Apostrophe to Form Possessives (Ownership), Comma Between Describing Words**

Steves family had a long bumpy flight over the mountains.

Week 30: Corrected Sentences

* **Italics and Underlining, Comma Between Items in a Series**

  <u>TV Guide</u> gives a table of times, channels, and programs for each night.

* **Italics and Underlining, Capitalization, Colon**

  We looked in the paper to see if <u>*G*ood *M*orning *A*merica</u> was on at 7:00 or 8:00.

* **Quotation Marks to Set Off Spoken Words, Comma to Set Off a Speaker's Words**

  "My little sister can read a stop sign," bragged Matthew.

* **Subject-Verb Agreement, Apostrophe in Contractions**

  Sue and Beth *are* going to the movies, and they'll come right home afterward.

* **Apostrophe to Form Possessives (Ownership), Comma Between Describing Words**

  Steve's family had a long, bumpy flight over the mountains.

Week 31: Mixed-Review Sentences

Science and Inventions 1

* Colon, Comma in Compound Sentences, Capitalization

Our assembly will begin at 130 and the speaker will tell us about some of Benjamin franklin's inventions.

* Capitalization, Subject-Verb Agreement

In 1931, the empire state building were the tallest building in the world.

* Apostrophe in Contractions, Comma to Keep Numbers Clear

I wouldnt want to wash the windows of the Empire State Building, because its 1250 feet tall!

* Apostrophe in Contractions, Run-On Sentence

Were lucky that vaccines have been developed many people would have died without them.

* Hyphen, Capitalization

Mars is about one half the size of earth.

Week 31: Corrected Sentences

✳ Colon, Comma in Compound Sentences, Capitalization

Our assembly will begin at 1:30, and the speaker will tell us about some of Benjamin Franklin's inventions.

✳ Capitalization, Subject-Verb Agreement

In 1931, the Empire State Building was the tallest building in the world.

✳ Apostrophe in Contractions, Comma to Keep Numbers Clear

I wouldn't want to wash the windows of the Empire State Building, because it's 1,250 feet tall!

✳ Apostrophe in Contractions, Run-On Sentence

We're lucky that vaccines have been developed. Many people would have died without them.

✳ Hyphen, Capitalization

Mars is about one-half the size of Earth.

MUG Shot Sentences

Week 32: Mixed-Review Sentences

Science and Inventions 2

✷ **Capitalization, Comma to Keep Numbers Clear, End Punctuation**

The Sears tower is 1454 feet tall

✷ **Capitalization, Adjective (Form)**

henry ford wanted to produce automobiles more faster than before.

✷ **Comma in Dates, Capitalization, Using the Right Word**

The Concorde made it's first flights to Paris, london, and New york on November 22 1977.

✷ **Capitalization, End Punctuation**

In 1957 the russians launched an orbiting satellite called *Sputnik*

✷ **Subject-Verb Agreement, Comma Between Describing Words**

Subways is train systems that travel underground through huge dark tunnels.

Week 32: Corrected Sentences

✱ **Capitalization, Comma to Keep Numbers Clear, End Punctuation**

The Sears *T*ower is 1,454 feet tall.

✱ **Capitalization, Adjective (Form)**

*H*enry *F*ord wanted to produce automobiles ~~more~~ faster than before.

✱ **Comma in Dates, Capitalization, Using the Right Word**

The Concorde made ~~it's~~ *its* first flights to Paris, *L*ondon, and New *Y*ork on November 22, 1977.

✱ **Capitalization, End Punctuation**

In 1957 the *R*ussians launched an orbiting satellite called *Sputnik*.

✱ **Subject-Verb Agreement, Comma Between Describing Words**

Subways ~~is~~ *are* train systems that travel underground through huge, dark tunnels.

MUG Shot Sentences

Week 33: Mixed-Review Sentences

Science and Inventions 3

* **Apostrophe to Form Possessives (Ownership), Capitalization**

   Samuel Morses great invention was the morse code.

* **Capitalization, Using the Right Word, End Punctuation**

   did you no that a sewing machine is used to bind books

* **Comma To Keep Numbers Clear, Run-On Sentence, Period After an Initial**

   In 1879 Thomas A Edison invented the lightbulb he made more than 1000 inventions in his lifetime.

* **Capitalization, Run-On Sentence**

   In 1793 Eli whitney invented the cotton gin in 1798 he invented mass production.

* **Using the Right Word, Apostrophe to Form Possessives (Ownership)**

   Scientists say there is a whole in the earths ozone layer.

Week 33: Corrected Sentences

* **Apostrophe to Form Possessives (Ownership), Capitalization**

    Samuel Morse's great invention was the Morse Code.

* **Capitalization, Using the Right Word, End Punctuation**

    Did you know that a sewing machine is used to bind books?

* **Comma To Keep Numbers Clear, Run-On Sentence, Period After an Initial**

    In 1879 Thomas A. Edison invented the lightbulb. He made more than 1,000 inventions in his lifetime.

* **Capitalization, Run-On Sentence**

    In 1793 Eli Whitney invented the cotton gin. In 1798 he invented mass production.

* **Using the Right Word, Apostrophe to Form Possessives (Ownership)**

    Scientists say there is a hole in the earth's ozone layer.

MUG Shot Sentences

Week 34: Mixed-Review Sentences

Literature and Life 1

✳ Run-On Sentence, Italics and Underlining

The first successful newspaper in America was published in 1704 it was called the Boston News-Letter.

✳ Italics and Underlining, Capitalization, Period After an Abbreviation

The Cat in the hat is a famous book by Dr Seuss.

✳ Capitalization, Comma Between a City and a State, Sentence Fragment

In 1757 streetlights were installed in philadelphia pennsylvania. Easier to see at night.

✳ Quotation Marks to Set Off Spoken Words, Capitalization, Period After an Abbreviation

america's first ice-cream company was founded in 1786, said Mr Thomas.

✳ Capitalization, Comma in Compound Sentences

The american bald eagle is the nation's symbol but Benjamin franklin wanted it to be the turkey.

Week 34: Corrected Sentences

* **Run-On Sentence, Italics and Underlining**

  The first successful newspaper in America was published in 1704. /It was called the <u>Boston News-Letter</u>.

* **Italics and Underlining, Capitalization, Period After an Abbreviation**

  The <u>Cat in the Hat</u> is a famous book by Dr. Seuss.

* **Capitalization, Comma Between a City and a State, Sentence Fragment**

  In 1757 streetlights were installed in Philadelphia, Pennsylvania. They made it easier to see at night.

* **Quotation Marks to Set Off Spoken Words, Capitalization, Period After an Abbreviation**

  "America's first ice-cream company was founded in 1786," said Mr. Thomas.

* **Capitalization, Comma in Compound Sentences**

  The American bald eagle is the nation's symbol, but Benjamin Franklin wanted it to be the turkey.

MUG Shot Sentences

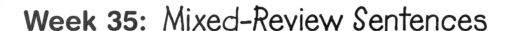

Week 35: Mixed-Review Sentences

Literature and Life 2

✳ **Apostrophe in Contractions, Quotation Marks to Punctuate Titles**

My mom cant sing the high notes in The Star-Spangled Banner, but she tries her best.

✳ **Italics and Underlining, Sentence Fragment,
Apostrophe to Form Possessives (Ownership)**

Lewis Carroll wrote Alices Adventures in Wonderland. Finished in 1865.

✳ **Period After an Initial, Colon, Comma Between Items in a Series**

L Frank Baum is the creator of these characters the Scarecrow the Cowardly Lion and the Tin Man.

✳ **Italics and Underlining, Run-On Sentence, Capitalization**

My brother reads the magazine Boys' Life it helps him in boy scouts.

✳ **Comma in Compound Sentences, Apostrophe in Contractions**

Robin Williams is in lots of funny movies and hes my favorite actor.

Week 35: Corrected Sentences

* **Apostrophe in Contractions, Quotation Marks to Punctuate Titles**

  My mom can't sing the high notes in "The Star-Spangled Banner," but she tries her best.

* **Italics and Underlining, Sentence Fragment,**
  Apostrophe to Form Possessives (Ownership)

  Lewis Carroll wrote Alice's Adventures in Wonderland. It was finished in 1865.

* **Period After an Initial, Colon, Comma Between Items in a Series**

  L. Frank Baum is the creator of these characters: the Scarecrow, the Cowardly Lion, and the Tin Man.

* **Italics and Underlining, Run-On Sentence, Capitalization**

  My brother reads the magazine Boys' Life. It helps him in Boy Scouts.

* **Comma in Compound Sentences, Apostrophe in Contractions**

  Robin Williams is in lots of funny movies, and he's my favorite actor.

MUG Shot Sentences

MUG Shot Paragraphs

The MUG Shot paragraphs are a quick and efficient way to review **m**echanics, **u**sage, and **g**rammar errors each week. These paragraphs can also serve as excellent proofreading exercises. Each paragraph can be corrected and discussed in 8 to 10 minutes.

Implementation and Evaluation

For each set of MUG Shot sentences, there is a corresponding MUG Shot paragraph. The first 15 weeks of MUG Shot paragraphs focus on the one or two skills addressed in each week's sentences. The remaining 20 weeks of paragraphs feature a mixed review of proofreading skills covered in each week's sentences.

Implementation

A MUG Shot paragraph can be implemented at the end of the week as a review or an evaluation activity. It may be done orally as a class. Otherwise you may simply distribute copies of the week's paragraph, read the paragraph aloud, and then have students make their corrections on the sheet. Students may use the "Editing and Proofreading Marks" in their handbooks or on page iv in this book. Have students discuss their changes (in pairs or in small groups). Afterward, go over the paragraph as a class to make sure that everyone understands the reasons for the changes. (You may want to refer to the corresponding MUG Shot sentences during your discussion.)

An Alternative Approach: Distribute copies of the MUG Shot paragraph along with the edited version. (They appear on the same page in your booklet.) Have students fold the edited version under, and then make their own changes. Once they are finished, they can unfold the paper and check their work.

Evaluation

If you use the paragraphs as an evaluation activity, we recommend that you give students a basic performance score for their work. This score should reflect the number of changes the student has marked correctly (before or after any discussion). The weekly score might also reflect the student's work on the corresponding MUG Shot sentences.

Note: In the MUG Shot paragraphs showing corrections for run-on sentences and sentence fragments, one possible correction is shown. However, there are often a number of possible answers that would also be correct.

WEEK 1: Underground Steam Engine

■ End Punctuation

Michael's family went out West last summer They saw Old Faithful It is a famous geyser Do you know what a geyser is It's a spring that shoots hot water and steam high into the air Whoosh Old Faithful sends water as high as a 15-story building Can you imagine that

WEEK 1: Corrected Paragraph

Michael's family went out West last summer. They saw Old Faithful. It is a famous geyser. Do you know what a geyser is? It's a spring that shoots hot water and steam high into the air. Whoosh! Old Faithful sends water as high as a 15-story building. Can you imagine that?

MUG Shot Paragraphs

WEEK 2: Good Books

■ **Period After an Initial and After an Abbreviation**

Our class visited the library at 325 S Birch St. Our teacher got a book about Winnie the Pooh. A A Milne is one of Ms Moy's favorite authors. She also got a book by C S Lewis. I got a book about Cal Ripken, Jr, and I got *Curious George,* by H A Rey. *Curious George* is for my little sister. I also got her a book called *Mr Gumpy's Outing.*

WEEK 2: Corrected Paragraph

Our class visited the library at 325 S. Birch St. Our teacher got a book about Winnie the Pooh. A. A. Milne is one of Ms. Moy's favorite authors. She also got a book by C. S. Lewis. I got a book about Cal Ripken, Jr., and I got *Curious George,* by H. A. Rey. *Curious George* is for my little sister. I also got her a book called *Mr. Gumpy's Outing.*

WEEK 3: The Great Outdoors

■ Comma Between Items in a Series

Jake has been to Michigan Wisconsin Ohio and Pennsylvania. He also has visited four of the Great Lakes: Superior Michigan Huron and Erie. Jake and his family go camping fishing and boating. Jake likes to take photos draw pictures and collect rocks.

WEEK 3: Corrected Paragraph

Jake has been to Michigan Wisconsin Ohio and Pennsylvania. He also has visited four of the Great Lakes: Superior Michigan Huron and Erie. Jake and his family go camping fishing and boating. Jake likes to take photos draw pictures and collect rocks.

MUG Shot Paragraphs

WEEK 4: Thousands of Seats

■ Comma to Keep Numbers Clear

Michigan Stadium can seat more than 106000 football fans! Most football stadiums seat between 60000 and 80000 people. Baseball stadiums are a little smaller. Busch Stadium in St. Louis seats 57000 people. Basketball arenas are even smaller. Most can seat between 16000 and 22000 people.

WEEK 4: Corrected Paragraph

Michigan Stadium can seat more than 106,000 football fans! Most football stadiums seat between 60,000 and 80,000 people. Baseball stadiums are a little smaller. Busch Stadium in St. Louis seats 57,000 people. Basketball arenas are even smaller. Most can seat between 16,000 and 22,000 people.

WEEK 5: Wish You Were Here

■ Comma in Dates and Between a City and a State

Darrin's Uncle Frank took a trip to Kitty Hawk North Carolina. That's where the Wright brothers flew the first airplane. The date was December 17 1903. Darrin's uncle visited there on December 17 2000. He also went to Virginia. He sent Darrin a postcard from Norfolk Virginia.

WEEK 5: Corrected Paragraph

Darrin's Uncle Frank took a trip to Kitty Hawk, North Carolina. That's where the Wright brothers flew the first airplane. The date was December 17, 1903. Darrin's uncle visited there on December 17, 2000. He also went to Virginia. He sent Darrin a postcard from Norfolk, Virginia.

WEEK 6: Hide-and-Seek Beans

■ Comma in Compound Sentences

We had lima beans for dinner but only Mom ate them. I buried mine under mashed potatoes and no one noticed. My sister dropped hers and our dog ate every one. I cleared the table and I found Dad's beans in his napkin. He's a grown-up but he still doesn't like lima beans!

WEEK 6: Corrected Paragraph

We had lima beans for dinner‸but only Mom ate them. I buried mine under mashed potatoes‸and no one noticed. My sister dropped hers‸and our dog ate every one. I cleared the table‸and I found Dad's beans in his napkin. He's a grown-up‸but he still doesn't like lima beans!

WEEK 7: All Alike

■ **Comma to Set Off a Speaker's Words**

"Hi, Victor" I said. "Want to ride bikes with my dad and me?"

"Sure" Victor answered. "I'll ask my mom."

Victor yelled "Mom, can I go biking with Josh and his dad?"

"Yes, but don't forget your helmet" his mom yelled back.

"Gee" I said to Victor "my mom said the same thing!"

WEEK 7: Corrected Paragraph

"Hi, Victor," I said. "Want to ride bikes with my dad and me?"

"Sure," Victor answered. "I'll ask my mom."

Victor yelled, "Mom, can I go biking with Josh and his dad?"

"Yes, but don't forget your helmet," his mom yelled back.

"Gee," I said to Victor, "my mom said the same thing!"

MUG Shot Paragraphs

WEEK 8: Good Books, Good Friends

■ Comma After an Introductory Word or Group of Words

"When you're done reading that book may I read it?"

"Sure I'll lend it to you."

"Chantal you are a good friend."

"After you finish the book please return it to me."

WEEK 8: Corrected Paragraph

"When you're done reading that book⌃may I read it?"

"Sure⌃I'll lend it to you."

"Chantal⌃you are a good friend."

"After you finish the book⌃please return it to me."

WEEK 9: A Big, Beautiful Garden

■ **Comma Between Describing Words**

We live on a wide shady street. Our house has a big grassy yard. In the back my dad grows red juicy tomatoes and colorful sweet-smelling roses. The tall thorny roses keep curious hungry animals out.

WEEK 9: Corrected Paragraph

We live on a wide‸shady street. Our house has a big‸grassy yard. In the back my dad grows red‸juicy tomatoes and colorful‸ sweet-smelling roses. The tall‸thorny roses keep curious‸hungry animals out.

MUG Shot Paragraphs

WEEK 10: Call It a Day

■ Colon

I had to do three chores on Saturday walk the dog, unload the dishwasher, and help with the laundry. My sister had two chores give the dog a bath and help wash the windows. We both finished at 1130. After lunch, we did our two favorite things played soccer at 200 and then watched videos.

WEEK 10: Corrected Paragraph

I had to do three chores on Saturday: walk the dog, unload the dishwasher, and help with the laundry. My sister had two chores: give the dog a bath and help wash the windows. We both finished at 11:30. After lunch, we did our two favorite things: played soccer at 2:00 and then watched videos.

WEEK 11: *Recess!*

■ **Apostrophe in Contractions**

Its time for recess. Were going to play kickball. We dont have time to finish a game, but that doesnt matter. Well continue the game tomorrow.

WEEK 11: Corrected Paragraph

It's time for recess. We're going to play kickball. We don't have time to finish a game, but that doesn't matter. We'll continue the game tomorrow.

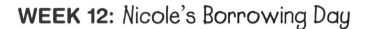

WEEK 12: Nicole's Borrowing Day

■ Apostrophe to Form Possessives (Ownership)

Nicole had to use Ramas spelling book to study her words. She borrowed Autumns math book and Dales markers. At recess she wore the teachers sweater. Then she shared a friends lunch. This all happened because her backpacks zipper was stuck!

WEEK 12: Corrected Paragraph

Nicole had to use Rama's spelling book to study her words. She borrowed Autumn's math book and Dale's markers. At recess she wore the teacher's sweater. Then she shared a friend's lunch. This all happened because her backpack's zipper was stuck!

WEEK 13: Girls' Dress-Up Day

■ Apostrophe to Form Possessives (Ownership)

My friends names are Lakeshia and Nadine. We like to dress up in our moms old dresses. We all have older sisters, and we borrow our sisters shoes. We love to wear Nadines two old aunts crazy hats. We wore our outfits to our brothers band concert.

WEEK 13: Corrected Paragraph

My friends' names are Lakeshia and Nadine. We like to dress up in our moms' old dresses. We all have older sisters, and we borrow our sisters' shoes. We love to wear Nadine's two old aunts' crazy hats. We wore our outfits to our brothers' band concert.

MUG Shot Paragraphs

WEEK 14: What About Rocky?

■ Quotation Marks to Set Off Spoken Words

Mom, can we take Rocky to the beach? Tommy asked.

Tommy, kittens don't go to the beach, Mom answered.

But Rocky will be lonely if we're gone all day, Tommy argued.

I have an idea, I said. Maybe Rocky can spend the day with Aunt Amy.

Okay, Mom said. Call Aunt Amy and see if she can keep Rocky today.

WEEK 14: Corrected Paragraph

"Mom, can we take Rocky to the beach?" Tommy asked.

"Tommy, kittens don't go to the beach," Mom answered.

"But Rocky will be lonely if we're gone all day," Tommy argued.

"I have an idea," I said. "Maybe Rocky can spend the day with Aunt Amy."

"Okay," Mom said. "Call Aunt Amy and see if she can keep Rocky today."

WEEK 15: *Ramona and Ralph*

■ Italics and Underlining

Beverly Cleary wrote Ramona the Pest and many other children's books. I have read Ramona the Brave and Ramona Forever. I listened to Ralph S. Mouse and The Mouse and the Motorcycle on cassettes. Now I am reading Runaway Ralph.

WEEK 15: Corrected Paragraph

Beverly Cleary wrote <u>Ramona the Pest</u> and many other children's books. I have read <u>Ramona the Brave</u> and <u>Ramona Forever</u>. I listened to <u>Ralph S. Mouse</u> and <u>The Mouse and the Motorcycle</u> on cassettes. Now I am reading <u>Runaway Ralph</u>.

MUG Shot Paragraphs

WEEK 16: The Problem with Pluto

■ **Apostrophe in Contractions, Using the Right Word**

I wouldnt go to Pluto because its two cold and too far away. Pluto is 3,660 million miles from the son. That explains why its sow cold. If I visited Pluto, Id have to where very warm close. I dont have a coat that is warm enough for 350 degrees below zero.

WEEK 16: Corrected Paragraph

I wouldn't go to Pluto because it's ~~two~~ *too* cold and too far away. Pluto is 3,660 million miles from the ~~son~~ *sun*. That explains why it's ~~sow~~ *so* cold. If I visited Pluto, I'd have to ~~where~~ *wear* very warm ~~close~~ *clothes*. I don't have a coat that is warm enough for 350 degrees below zero.

WEEK 17: Surrounded

■ Capitalization, Colon, Comma Between Items in a Series

Many countries make up north america Canada the United States mexico and the Central American countries. Three oceans surround north america the arctic the pacific and the atlantic. The arctic Ocean is to the north, with the north pole at its center. The Pacific Ocean is to the west. The atlantic is to the east.

WEEK 17: Corrected Paragraph

Many countries make up *N*orth *A*merica: Canada, the United States, *M*exico, and the Central American countries. Three oceans surround *N*orth *A*merica: the *A*rctic, the *P*acific, and the *A*tlantic. The *A*rctic Ocean is to the north, with the *N*orth *P*ole at its center. The Pacific Ocean is to the west. The *A*tlantic is to the east.

MUG Shot Paragraphs

WEEK 18: The Beehive State

■ **Subject-Verb Agreement, Comma in Compound Sentences, Capitalization**

We was in Utah on our vacation and we floated in the great salt lake. It is just north of salt lake city and it contain 6 billion tons of salt. We also saw native american cliff dwellings and we visited rainbow bridge. It are the world's largest natural rock bridge.

WEEK 18: Corrected Paragraph

We ~~was~~ *were* in Utah on our vacation_∧_and we floated in the *G*reat *S*alt *L*ake. It is just north of *S*alt *L*ake *C*ity_∧_and it ~~contain~~ *contains* 6 billion tons of salt. We also saw *N*ative *A*merican cliff dwellings_∧_and we visited *R*ainbow *B*ridge. It ~~are~~ *is* the world's largest natural rock bridge.

WEEK 19: A Long, Wet Ride

■ Using the Right Word, Capitalization

Pioneers crossed many rivers and creaks as they traveled to oregon and california. Their were know bridges at that time. The pioneers took the wheels off there wagons and pushed them across rivers on rafts. They crossed the ohio, missouri, and other rivers this weigh. The oregon trail was often a watery rode!

WEEK 19: Corrected Paragraph

Pioneers crossed many rivers and ~~creaks~~ *creeks* as they traveled to ~~o~~*O*regon and ~~c~~*C*alifornia. ~~Their~~ *There* were ~~know~~ *no* bridges at that time. The pioneers took the wheels off ~~there~~ *their* wagons and pushed them across rivers on rafts. They crossed the ~~o~~*O*hio, ~~m~~*M*issouri, and other rivers this ~~weigh~~ *way*. The ~~o~~*O*regon ~~t~~*T*rail was often a watery ~~rode~~ *road*!

MUG Shot Paragraphs

WEEK 20: Flying High

■ **Comma After an Introductory Group of Words, Verb (Irregular), Capitalization**

When he flied across the atlantic ocean in 1927 Charles Lindbergh became a hero. He beginned his trip on the morning of may 20. "lucky lindy" took off from new york, headed for Paris. It taked him more than 33 hours to get there. His plane circled the eiffel tower and landed safely.

WEEK 20: Corrected Paragraph

When he ~~flied~~ *flew* across the **A**tlantic **O**cean in 1927, Charles Lindbergh became a hero. He ~~beginned~~ *began* his trip on the morning of **M**ay 20. "**L**ucky **L**indy" took off from **N**ew **Y**ork, headed for Paris. It ~~taked~~ *took* him more than 33 hours to get there. His plane circled the **E**iffel **T**ower and landed safely.

WEEK 21: Edison's Life

■ Plurals, Capitalization, Comma in Compound Sentences

Leroy looked for two biographys of thomas edison but he found only one. It was a good one and he found lots of interesting factes. Edison worked in menlo park, new jersey and he made more than 1,000 inventions. Besides lightbulbes, he invented new kinds of batterys and cameras.

WEEK 21: Corrected Paragraph

Leroy looked for two ~~biographys~~ *biographies* of ~~t~~*T*homas ~~e~~*E*dison,/but he found only one. It was a good one,/and he found lots of interesting ~~factes~~ *facts*. Edison worked in ~~m~~*M*enlo ~~p~~*P*ark, ~~n~~*N*ew ~~j~~*J*ersey,/and he made more than 1,000 inventions. Besides ~~lightbulbes~~ *lightbulbs*, he invented new kinds of ~~batterys~~ *batteries* and cameras.

MUG Shot Paragraphs

WEEK 22: Dr. Seuss

■ **Period After an Abbreviation, Italics and Underlining, Capitalization**

Dr Seuss was the author of Green eggs and Ham. He also wrote The cat in the hat, fox in socks, and lots of other books. Dr Seuss's real name was mr theodor seuss geisel. He won many awards, including the pulitzer prize and three Academy Awards. My favorite Dr Seuss book is how the grinch stole Christmas.

WEEK 22: Corrected Paragraph

Dr. Seuss was the author of <u>Green **E**ggs and Ham</u>. He also wrote <u>The **C**at in the **H**at</u>, <u>**F**ox in **S**ocks</u>, and lots of other books. Dr. Seuss's real name was **M**r. **T**heodor **S**euss **G**eisel. He won many awards, including the **P**ulitzer **P**rize and three Academy Awards. My favorite Dr. Seuss book is <u>**H**ow the **G**rinch **S**tole Christmas</u>.

WEEK 23: The Whole Enchilada

■ **Capitalization, Comma Between Items in a Series**

There are french german and spanish words in our language. *City state* and *nation* all come from french. *Book hamburger* and *pretzel* come from german. *Taco cigar* and *mosquito* come from spanish. You can probably think of more words we have borrowed from spanish.

WEEK 23: Corrected Paragraph

There are ~~f~~**F**rench**,** ~~g~~**G**erman**,** and ~~s~~**S**panish words in our language. *City***,** *state***,** and *nation* all come from ~~f~~**F**rench. *Book***,** *hamburger***,** and *pretzel* come from ~~g~~**G**erman. *Taco***,** *cigar***,** and *mosquito* come from ~~s~~**S**panish. You can probably think of more words we have borrowed from ~~s~~**S**panish.

MUG Shot Paragraphs

WEEK 24: Books by Hand

■ **Capitalization, Using the Right Word**

the first printed books were maid in london in the 1400s. before that, someone had to right out every book by hand. most people could not afford to by books because they cost to much. it could take a weak or more to copy a hole book. The person who did the copying had to be paid four all that work.

WEEK 24: Corrected Paragraph

T
/the first printed books were ~~maid~~ *made* in /*L*ondon in the 1400s. /*B*efore

write
that, someone had to ~~right~~ out every book by hand. /*M*ost people

buy *too* *I*
could not afford to ~~by~~ books because they cost ~~to~~ much. /t could take

week *whole*
a ~~weak~~ or more to copy a ~~hole~~ book. The person who did the

for
copying had to be paid ~~four~~ all that work.

WEEK 25: A Plain Plane

■ Comma Between Items in a Series, Run-On Sentence

Words like *through though* and *tough* are hard to learn they look like they should rhyme. *So sew* and *sow* look like they should sound different they sound alike, except that *sow* can be said two different ways. Here are more spellings that can be said two ways: *tear lead bass close does*. Each of these spells two different words the two words have completely different meanings.

WEEK 25: Corrected Paragraph

Words like *through*‸ *though*‸ and *tough* are hard to learn. They look like they should rhyme. *So*‸ *sew*‸ and *sow* look like they should sound different. They sound alike, except that *sow* can be said two different ways. Here are more spellings that can be said two ways: *tear*‸ *lead*‸ *bass*‸ *close*‸ *does*. Each of these spells two different words. The two words have completely different meanings.

MUG Shot Paragraphs

WEEK 26: Beginning French

■ Quotation Marks to Set Off Spoken Words, Comma to Set Off a Speaker's Words

Bonjour said the French visitor.

Uh, I don't speak French I answered.

It's easy he said. *Bonjour* means hello.

Bonjour I repeated. My name is Michelle.

You do speak French he said with a smile. Michelle is a French

name.

WEEK 26: Corrected Paragraph

"*Bonjour*," said the French visitor.

"Uh, I don't speak French," I answered.

"It's easy," he said. "*Bonjour* means hello."

"*Bonjour*," I repeated. "My name is Michelle."

"You do speak French," he said with a smile. "Michelle is a French

name."

WEEK 27: Measure Twice

■ Quotation Marks to Set Off Spoken Words, Hyphen

There are about two and one half centimeters in one inch, said Mr. Anderson.

A penny is about three quarters of an inch wide, he continued, so it is about two centimeters. A quarter is about one inch wide. How many centimeters is that?

Two and one half centimeters, Christy said.

Right! said Mr. Anderson.

WEEK 27: Corrected Paragraph

"There are about two and one-half centimeters in one inch," said Mr. Anderson.

"A penny is about three-quarters of an inch wide," he continued, "so it is about two centimeters. A quarter is about one inch wide. How many centimeters is that?"

"Two and one-half centimeters," Christy said.

"Right!" said Mr. Anderson.

MUG Shot Paragraphs

WEEK 28: Picture This

■ **Using the Right Word, Sentence Fragment**

The heart symbol stands four a feeling. Means love. The dove and the olive branch are both symbols for piece. Some rode signs have symbols. A leaping dear. A person walking.

WEEK 28: Corrected Paragraph

The heart symbol stands ~~four~~ *for* a feeling. *It m*/Means love. The dove and the olive branch are both symbols for ~~piece~~ *peace*. Some ~~rode~~ *road* signs have symbols. *One is a*/A leaping ~~dear~~ *deer* *Another one is a*/A person walking.

WEEK 29: Pet Count

■ **Rambling Sentence, Apostrophe in Contractions**

I had to do a survey and I couldnt decide what to do so I asked my teacher and she said shed like to know about everyone's pets. Five kids have fish and four kids have hamsters and eight kids have dogs and three kids dont have any pets.

WEEK 29: Corrected Paragraph

I had to do a survey, and I couldn't decide what to do. So I asked my teacher, and she said she'd like to know about everyone's pets. Five kids have fish, four kids have hamsters, eight kids have dogs, and three kids don't have any pets.

WEEK 30: At the Movies

■ **Subject-Verb Agreement, Apostrophe in Contractions**

Sue and Beth is going to the movies, and then theyll come right home. They goes to the movies every Saturday. If they cant find a movic they wants to see, they goes to one they have already seen. Sometimes they sees the same movie three times.

WEEK 30: Corrected Paragraph

Sue and Beth ~~is~~ *are* going to the movies, and then they'll come right home. They ~~goes~~ *go* to the movies every Saturday. If they can't find a movie they ~~wants~~ *want* to see, they ~~goes~~ *go* to one they have already seen. Sometimes they ~~sees~~ *see* the same movie three times.

WEEK 31: All About Ben

■ Colon, Comma in Compound Sentences, Capitalization

Our assembly will begin at 130 and the speaker will tell us about some of Benjamin franklin's inventions. The speaker's name is rosa franklin but she is not related to Ben. I know that he invented these things the Franklin stove and the lightning rod. I'm sure we'll learn about more inventions. At 230 we will go back to class and we will write about what we learned.

WEEK 31: Corrected Paragraph

Our assembly will begin at 1:30 and the speaker will tell us about some of Benjamin Franklin's inventions. The speaker's name is Rosa Franklin, but she is not related to Ben. I know that he invented these things: the Franklin stove and the lightning rod. I'm sure we'll learn about more inventions. At 2:30 we will go back to class, and we will write about what we learned.

MUG Shot Paragraphs

WEEK 32: Ford's Biggest Idea

■ **Capitalization, Adjective (Form)**

henry ford wanted to produce automobiles more faster than before. That would make them more cheaper to build and more easier to afford. ford's model t was the successfullest car of its time. henry ford once worked for thomas edison, another great inventor.

WEEK 32: Corrected Paragraph

      H   F
Henry **f**ord wanted to produce automobiles ~~more~~ faster than before. That would make them ~~more~~ cheaper to build and ~~more~~ easier to afford. **F**ord's **m**odel **t** was the ~~successfullest~~ *most successful* car of its time. **H**enry **f**ord once worked for **t**homas **e**dison, another great inventor.

WEEK 33: Dot, Dot, Dash

■ **Apostrophe to Form Possessives (Ownership), Capitalization**

Samuel Morses great invention was the morse code. The inventors helper, alexander bain, helped create the code. The telegraph was also Morses invention. The countrys first telegraph line ran from washington, D.C., to baltimore, maryland.

WEEK 33: Corrected Paragraph

Samuel Morse's great invention was the **M**orse **C**ode. The inventor's helper, **A**lexander **B**ain, helped create the code. The telegraph was also Morse's invention. The country's first telegraph line ran from **W**ashington, D.C., to **B**altimore, **M**aryland.

MUG Shot Paragraphs

WEEK 34: A Popular Bird

■ **Capitalization, Comma in Compound Sentences**

The american bald eagle was chosen as a U.S. symbol but Benjamin franklin wanted the turkey to be chosen. The eagle was a good choice for it has long been a symbol of power and strength. Rulers in ancient egypt used the eagle as a symbol and napoleon had one on his flag.

WEEK 34: Corrected Paragraph

The *A*/american bald eagle was chosen as a U.S. symbol‚but Benjamin *F*/franklin wanted the turkey to be chosen. The eagle was a good choice‚for it has long been a symbol of power and strength. Rulers in ancient *E*/egypt used the eagle as a symbol‚and *N*/napoleon had one on his flag.

WEEK 35: Oh, Say, Can You Sing?

■ **Apostrophe in Contractions, Quotation Marks to Punctuate Titles, Capitalization**

My mom cant sing the high notes in The Star-spangled Banner, but she tries her best. She says shed be happier if america the beautiful were our national anthem. Its easier to sing, she says. Dad says row, row, row your boat is easy, but that doesnt make it a good anthem.

WEEK 35: Corrected Paragraph

My mom can't sing the high notes in "The Star-Spangled Banner," but she tries her best. She says she'd be happier if "America the Beautiful" were our national anthem. It's easier to sing, she says. Dad says "Row, Row, Row Your Boat" is easy, but that doesn't make it a good anthem.

Daily Writing Practice

This section offers three types of writing practice. The freewriting done in response to the **writing prompts** can be shared in follow-up sessions and later shaped into finished writing. The discussion of daily journal writing introduces lists of **writing topics.** The topics address a wide range of writing ideas. Finally, "showing" in writing, developed by expanding on the **Show-Me sentences,** can be shared in follow-up sessions and later shaped into finished descriptive paragraphs.

A Writing Prompts Question-and-Answer Sheet

You may duplicate the following question-and-answer information about writing prompts as a handout for students or use it as the basis for a class discussion.

Anyone who wants to be a good writer has to practice often. That's why so many writers keep journals and diaries. That's why your teacher might ask you to write something nearly every day in school. Sometime your teacher might ask you to use a writing prompt.

A writing prompt can be anything that gets you thinking and writing. It can be a question, a picture, or a title. When you see the prompt, you write whatever comes to your mind. And you keep writing until your thoughts are all gone. That's it!

How do I get started? It's really very simple. You just write down whatever comes into your mind when you think about your writing prompt.

Should I plan what I'm going to write about? No, don't try to plan anything. That's the whole idea. Just write. Be surprised by what you write.

What can I do to keep my writing going? Don't stop! When you run out of ideas, try thinking about your topic in a new way. For example, you might compare your topic to something else.

When should I stop? If you are doing a timed writing (about 5-10 minutes), stop when the time is up. Or you might decide it's time to stop when you fill up one page.

What do I do with my writing? You might share it with a classmate and see what she or he thinks. Or you can show it to a friend or to your mom or dad. Or you might use it later when you need a topic for a writing assignment.

So, really, all I have to do is start writing? Right!

Daily Writing Practice

WRITING PROMPT

If I were a . . .

_____

_____

_____

_____

_____

_____

_____

_____

_____

_____

_____

_____

Daily Writing Practice

WRITING PROMPT

When I was in kindergarten . . .

_____

_____

_____

_____

_____

_____

_____

_____

_____

_____

Daily Writing Practice

WRITING PROMPT

What do animals at the zoo think of people?

Daily Writing Practice

WRITING PROMPT

If I opened the treasure box . . .

_____

_____

_____

_____

_____

_____

_____

_____

_____

_____

_____

_____

_____

_____

Daily Writing Practice

WRITING PROMPT

If I could spend a day at the beach ...

_____

_____

_____

_____

_____

_____

_____

_____

_____

_____

_____

Daily Writing Practice

WRITING PROMPT

If my shoes could talk . . .

_____

_____

_____

_____

_____

_____

_____

_____

WRITING PROMPT

Taking Care of a Pet

_____

_____

_____

_____

_____

_____

_____

_____

_____

_____

_____

_____

_____

Daily Writing Practice

WRITING PROMPT

Times for Good Manners

_____

_____

_____

_____

_____

_____

_____

_____

_____

_____

_____

_____

_____

_____

_____

_____

Daily Writing Practice

WRITING PROMPT (Draw your snack.)

How to Make a Special Snack

_____

_____

_____

_____

_____

_____

_____

_____

Daily Writing Practice

WRITING PROMPT
Draw a place you would like to visit. Then write about the place.

WRITING PROMPT

Around the Campfire

_____

_____

_____

_____

_____

_____

_____

_____

_____

_____

_____

_____

_____

WRITING PROMPT

It's time to celebrate!

_____

_____

_____

_____

_____

_____

_____

_____

_____

_____

_____

_____

_____

_____

Daily Writing Practice

WRITING PROMPT

Directions for Getting to My Castle

_____

_____

_____

_____

_____

_____

_____

_____

_____

_____

Daily Writing Practice

WRITING PROMPT

People Who Lived Long Ago

_____

_____

_____

_____

_____

_____

_____

_____

_____

WRITING PROMPT

When these rakes started dancing . . .

_____

_____

_____

_____

_____

_____

_____

_____

_____

_____

_____

_____

Daily Writing Practice

WRITING PROMPT

Sometimes I feel...

Daily Writing Practice

WRITING PROMPT
Sailing Away

_____

_____

_____

_____

_____

_____

_____

_____

_____

_____

_____

_____

Daily Writing Practice

WRITING PROMPT

Ways I Have Fun

_____

_____

_____

_____

_____

_____

_____

_____

_____

_____

_____

_____

_____

Daily Writing Practice

WRITING PROMPT

When I see lightning . . .

_____

_____

_____

_____

_____

_____

_____

_____

_____

_____

_____

Daily Writing Practice

WRITING PROMPT

My friends and I like . . .

_____

_____

_____

_____

_____

_____

_____

_____

_____

_____

_____

_____

_____

Daily Writing Practice

WRITING PROMPT

Every winter I like to . . .

_____

_____

_____

_____

_____

_____

_____

_____

_____

_____

_____

_____

Daily Writing Practice

WRITING PROMPT

When I grow up . . .

_____

_____

_____

_____

_____

_____

_____

_____

_____

_____

_____

_____

Daily Writing Practice

Writing Topics
Daily Journal Writing

> "I can tap into [my students'] human instinct to write if I help them realize that their lives and memories are worth telling stories about, and if I help them zoom in on topics of fundamental importance to them."
>
> **—writing teacher JUNE GOULD**

As classroom teachers, we know from firsthand experience that the personal stories young learners love to share can serve as the basis of an effective and lively writing program. Here's how we did it.

Getting Started

At the beginning of the school year, we introduced in-class journal writing to the students. We knew that the most effective way to get students into writing was simply to let them write often and freely about their own lives, without having to worry about grades or turning their writing in. This helped them develop a feel for "real" writing—writing that comes from their own thoughts and feelings.

That's where the journals come in. Nothing gets students into writing more effectively than a personal journal. (And no other type of writing is so easy to implement.) All your students need are spiral notebooks, pens, time to write, and encouragement to explore whatever is on their minds. (See pages 77-79 in the *Write on Track* handbook for more information.)

 We provided our students with four or five personal writing topics each time they wrote. They could use one of these topics as a starting point, or write about something else entirely. The choice was theirs. (We found that providing writing topics was easier and more productive than just saying "You've got plenty to write about.")

Writing Topics

To start off an exercise, we posted suggested writing topics like these:

- your most memorable kitchen-related experience,
- your favorite time of the day,
- coping with brothers or sisters,
- the day of the big storm, or
- what you did over the weekend.

Students would either choose from the list or write on a topic they preferred. See pages 141-142 in this booklet for more suggested topics. We asked our students to write every other day for the first 5-10 minutes of the class period. (Every Monday, Wednesday, and Friday were writing days.) Of course, we had to adjust our schedule at times, but, for the most part, the students wrote three times a week.

Keeping It Going

After everyone was seated and roll was taken, the journals were passed out, the topics were given, and everyone wrote. We expected students to write for a full 5-10 minutes, nonstop. They knew that they would earn a quarterly grade based on their participation in the journal writing.

> "Over the last fifteen years, a number of teachers around the country and their students have been amazed by what happened when people write ten to fifteen minutes without worrying about grammar, spelling, or punctuation, and concentrate only on telling some kind of truth."
>
> **—KEN MACRORIE**

Wrapping It Up

On days that we weren't writing, we shared some journal entries. Many writers chose to show their entries. For those who were reluctant, we encouraged them to read a favorite part or a funny line. The students loved these readings and the discussions that followed.

Personal Experience Papers

Periodically, we would interrupt the normal course of journal writing and sharing and make formal writing assignments. That is, we would meet with students to review their entries and select one (or part of one) to develop into a more polished writing. Usually, those entries that others enjoyed hearing and wanted to know more about would be the ones the young writers would choose to develop.

We wanted to make sure that their writing went through at least one or two thorough revisions, so we gave our writers plenty of class time to work on their papers. We also required them to turn in all preliminary work with their final drafts. (See "Writing Personal Narratives," pages 82-85, in the *Write on Track* handbook for guidelines for this type of writing.)

The experience papers were shared with the entire class at the end of the project. This was a fun and informal activity, but one that students came to appreciate as an important part of the entire composing process. It was their day. They were on stage. They were sharing the culmination of all their hard work—a special moment in their own lives.

Writing Topics

At School

I like my classroom because . . .
My favorite part of school is . . .
I have trouble with . . .
Our class read a book about . . .
During recess . . .
Next year I will . . .
Something I learned this week is . . .
I enjoyed our field trip to . . .

At Home

When I wake up . . .
At dinner last night . . .
My mom is nice because . . .
After school, when I get home . . .
My favorite thing in my room is . . .
I'd like to have a _____ for a pet.
When I have to study . . .
When Grandpa or Grandma calls . . .
The Oldest Thing in My Home

This is how I feel when . . .

I write a good story.
my mom or dad surprises me.
I get what I wished for.
I sing.
I get hurt.
I get an A on my report card.
school's out for the summer.
Grandma comes to the school concert.
the leaves turn colors.
winter is over.
it is raining.
I see a rainbow.
I get angry.

Describe

A place I like to be alone
A strange dream
Someone special
Something that is special to me
A machine
A great place to eat
Somewhere I'd like to go
A family party
The weather

A Big IF

If I was invisible . . .
If I could go anywhere . . .
If I could be any animal . . .
If I had a million dollars . . .
If I could change one thing about
    myself . . .
If I was the teacher . . .
If I could invent something . . .

I wonder . . .

what my first job will be.
why whales don't sink.
if there is life on other planets.
what people will wear in the year
    2100.
why people are mean to each other.
how big jets are able to fly.
where worms go in the winter.
how people kept track of time before
    there were clocks.
who my mother's friends were when
    she was my age.
what the future will be like.
what I will be famous for.
how I'd like living in the desert.

Daily Writing Practice

My Neighborhood

A Neighborhood Story
On My Way Home from School
A Letter in the Mail for Me
The People Who Work in My
    Neighborhood
A Conversation with My Neighbor
_____
This makes my neighborhood
    different from others.
Pets and Other Animals in My
    Neighborhood
I'd like my neighborhood better if . . .
The Best Playground

All About Me

What I Like About Myself
Something Most People Don't Know
My Favorite Thing to Do on Saturday
What My Mom and Dad Say About
    Me
Something I Am Good At
My Favorites: Foods, Colors, Games
My Favorite Time of Day
My Worst Time of Day

Incredible!

When I opened the door . . .
The wind blew a _____ into my yard!
All of a sudden, gravity stopped
    working!
The Magic Feather
I heard this noise and . . .
You'll never guess what I saw in our
aquarium.
On my way to Mars . . .
My pet started talking to me!
A Dinosaur Adventure

Mixed Bag

I wondered why no one was talking
    to me.
My Own Flag
One Special Day
A Dark, Scary Night
I was the star of a TV show.
Our School Princi-PAL
Things with Wings
I designed my own car.

Sports

A "good sport" is someone who . . .
I can explain how this sport is played.
A New Cheer for Our School
Winning and Losing
Rules for My Own Game
A Fan Letter to a Sports Star
The Game the *(sports team animal)*
    Played Against *(another sports*
    team animal)

My Senses

Smells I Like
My Favorite Recipe
Interesting Sounds
I see this when I close my eyes.
A Noisy Poem
This music makes me feel . . .
What do colors say?
What I See When I'm Upside Down
Sounds of Nature
Music to My Ears
A Scene to Remember
Scenic View
House Noises
Animal Sounds

Show-Me Sentences
Producing Writing with Details

Teachers have always said to their students, "Your writing needs details" or "This idea is too general." We even know of a teacher who had a special stamp made: "Give more examples."

So how should this problem be approached? It's obvious that simply telling students to add more details and examples is not enough. Even showing them how professional writers develop their ideas is not enough (although this does help). Students learn to add substance and depth to their writing through regular practice.

Here's one method that has worked for many students and teachers: the Show-Me sentences. Students begin with a basic topic—"My locker is messy," for example—and create a paragraph or brief essay that *shows* rather than *tells*. The sentence is a springboard for lively writing.

About Your Show-Me Sentences . . .

The following pages contain 45 Show-Me sentences. Each sentence speaks directly to students, so they should have little difficulty creating essays full of personal details. Again, we suggest that you use these sentences every other day for an extended period of time (at least a month).

Note: By design, each page of Show-Me sentences can be made into an overhead transparency.

Implementation

DAY ONE Before you ask students to work on their own, develop a Show-Me sentence as a class. Write a sample sentence on the board. Have students volunteer specific details that give this basic thought some life. List their ideas on the board. Next, construct a brief paragraph on the board using some of these details. (Make no mention of the original sentence in your paragraph.) Discuss the results. Make sure that your students see how specific details help create a visual image for the reader. Also have your students read and react to examples of "showing writing" from professional texts. (Share the sample of "showing writing" on page 144 with your students.)

DAY TWO Have students work on their first Show-Me sentences in class. Upon completion of their writing, have pairs of students share the results of their work. Then ask for volunteers to share their writing with the entire class.

DAY THREE Ask students to develop a new paragraph. At the beginning of the *next* class period, discuss the results (break into pairs as before). Continue in this fashion for a month.

Note: Reserve the first 5-10 minutes of each class period for writing or discussing. (Students who don't finish their writing in class should have it ready for the next day.)

Evaluation

Have students reserve a section in their notebooks for their writing or have them compile their work in a folder. At regular intervals, give them some type of performance score (a check, for example) for their efforts. At the end of the unit, have them select one or two of their best examples to revise and then submit for a thorough evaluation.

Sample Show-Me Writing

✳ **The bunny was so cute!**

The bunny was as soft as my mom's hair. It had black and white fur and dark brown eyes. Its small, pink nose twitched at me. Its ears stood straight up as it stood on its hind legs in its cage to get a better look around. It was a dwarf rabbit, so it would never get very big. I could easily hold it in two hands.

Show-Me Sentences

* **The doll was pretty.**

* **It was a windy day.**

* **Going to the beach is fun.**

* **The cat meowed loudly.**

* **He looked happy.**

Daily Writing Practice

Show-Me Sentences

✳ **Our new house is nice.**

✳ **Tacos are good.**

✳ **This food smells funny.**

✳ **His haircut is cool.**

✳ **I like the 4th of July.**

Show-Me Sentences

* **She walked slowly.**

* **The forest is shady.**

* **My dad likes sports.**

* **The dog does tricks.**

* **I like cooking.**

Daily Writing Practice

Show-Me Sentences

* **My bike is wonderful.**

* **We had a fine time at the playground.**

* **Birds were at the feeder.**

* **I enjoy doing things on the computer.**

* **Flowers are lovely.**

Show-Me Sentences

* **The baby cried.**

* **I got a gift for my birthday.**

* **It was a delicious dinner.**

* **Her voice sounds sad.**

* **He is wearing a bright shirt.**

Daily Writing Practice

Show-Me Sentences

* The machine made a lot of noise.

* The children were excited.

* The road is rough.

* The traffic is busy.

* I enjoy drawing.

Show-Me Sentences

* **That is a tall building.**

* **Dad was mad.**

* **A fire is colorful.**

* **The girl's face is dirty.**

* **This room is plain.**

Daily Writing Practice

Show-Me Sentences

✳ **The squirrel ran away.**

✳ **The store clerk was upset.**

✳ **The boy got hurt.**

✳ **Grandma is a kind woman.**

✳ **Those apples look good.**

Show-Me Sentences

✳ **We waited for a long time.**

✳ **The sunrise is beautiful.**

✳ **The test was hard.**

✳ **The stuffed animal is small.**

✳ **We had fun at the pool.**

Daily Writing Practice